OVER 100 ANSWERS
TO
NAGGING QUESTIONS ABOUT
PROPERTY INVESTMENT IN
NIGERIA

Mojisola Afolayan

© Mojisola Afolayan 2020

ISBN: 978-978-981-761-0

Published by

Daneliherald Communications (Print Doctor Africa)
Plot 15 Block B Road 411, OPIC Estate Agbara
www.printdoctorafrica.com

Dedication

This book is dedicated to God Almighty

Acknowledgements

The world is a better place!

Thanks to people who want to develop and lead others. What makes it even better are people who share the gift of their time to mentor future leaders they make the world a better place for us all.

To all the individuals I have had the opportunity to lead, be led by, or watch their leadership from afar, I want to say thank you for being the inspiration and foundation for my new book.

I want to thank my Mentors who constantly push, inspire and believe in me– Victor Ayeye, Muriel Thiam, Adefunke Adeyemi, Nonso Onye _Ezeh, Debo Adejana, and the great Akin Olawore of blessed Memory.

Having an idea and turning it into a book is as hard as it sounds. The experience is both internally challenging and rewarding. I especially want to thank the individuals that helped make this happen. Complete thanks to my coach Padebi Ojomo for recommending the great team who help me out with this book, Philip, Joseph, Mrs. Adedolapo the Chief editor and Mr. Ayodeji the print doctor.

I want to thank my family, I want to specially thank my darling Mother Alh F.A Yakubu, my children for their co-operation as well as their nannies over the period especially at night when I was writing and collating this book.

Finally I want to thank my Husband Oluwafemi Afolayan- Thank you for being a supportive Partner I trust, honor, and respect.

Thank you to everyone who strives to grow and help others grow

ABOUT THE BOOK:

Nigeria is West Africa's unrivalled economic powerhouse. With a population of over 190 million people and a gross domestic product of over US$380bn, Nigeria is Africa's most populous country and second largest economy. This is a great indication that the opportunities in Nigeria are endless and real estate is one of the avenue for investment opportunities.

This book *"Over 100 Answers to Nagging questions About Real Estate Investment in Nigeria"* written by leading property expert- ESV. Mojisola Afolayan ANIVS, RSV reveals in a simplified way- *the things you need to know and can do to invest safely in real estate in Nigeria without being exhausted*. Written in very simple language, you'll find answers to your most important nagging property questions, including…

- What is real estate itself?
- Who are the real estate professionals?
- What are the different title documents?
- How do I cope with issues regarding to ownership and possession?
  You will find answers to questions as simple as what is a square meter ….

There is no doubt this book is a property solution book; full of knowledge. I am sure you agree with me that without knowledge, action is useless. At the end of our days, we all want to build wealth through property however we must have property investment knowledge first

If your goal is to invest in property, remain happy, have a healthy life, made a difference and have peace of mind then this book *"Over 100 Answers to Nagging Questions about Real Estate in Nigeria"* will *show you how.*

Feedback

"This is a highly informative and inspiring book, Mojisola has made the world of property investing more accessible for beginners".

She has always demonstrated to be a pacesetter, a trailblazer. She is truly a motivation to many....

Oluwafemi Afolayan

Table of Contents

Introduction

I want to state that when you are looking for property to invest in, you need to be flexible, so you don't miss out on opportunities. More often than not, many people's budget cannot get them what they want in the area they want. You need to be open minded and careful as you search and to be cognizant that time is money as well. Greed is the main factor why many people get duped in real estate; this is because they want more than they should get ordinarily and the scammers are aware of this "greed", so they give you what you want and you play easily into their hands. Once again, I say 'buyers beware', seek professional advice, get your own independent search, focus on getting and building on your knowledge, and obey your instincts as you make a decision.

Having this book does not replace seeking professional guidance, it is to equip you and shed adequate light on your property acquisition knowledge. Whether you are a prospective investor, first home buyer, a property investor or a portfolio builder, you will find these information useful:

- ✓ Understanding land documents
- ✓ Know your professionals

- ✓ Keeping it simple
- ✓ Dealing with others
- ✓ Handling practicalities
- ✓ Making it last

This is an essential book tailored to equip you with valuable knowledge, answering the basic everyday questions every property investor or realtor should know about property.

1

UNDERSTANDING BASIC TERMS

1. What is Land?

Land is the solid part of the earth's surface. All around the world, there is great demand for land and it is limited in supply; hence the reason its prices increase on a daily basis. Land, sometimes referred to as dry land, is the solid surface of Earth that is not permanently covered by water. The vast majority of human activity throughout history has occurred in land areas that support agriculture, habitat, and various natural resources.

Land is an essential input and factor of production which cannot be consumed. When you use the term land, it includes all the physical elements that serve as the wealth of a nation, which comprises the weather, forests, climate, mountains, hills, valley, and the entire environment. This is the lowest cadre and an easy entry point on the property ladder when talking about property investment.

2.   What is Real Estate?

Real estate is simply "Property" which consists of both the land and buildings on it including everything beneath and above it such as crops, minerals, and the air space. Real estate is another term for property, it is the real or physical property, and it is tangible. Real estate relates to land and anything immovable attached to the land itself.

3.   What is Property Investment?

It is the real estate property that has been purchased with the intention of earning a return on the investment either through rental income or the future resale of the property or both. It is simply the purchase, ownership, management, rental or sale of real estate for profit in the future.

Investing in property is generally a great investment option when done properly with the right clarity and understanding. It can generate ongoing passive income and can be a good long term investment, especially because the values tend to increase over time. Property investment is a big deal and if done properly can become highly lucrative. Although in many cases, you will need to put down a significant amount of money upfront when you want to begin real estate investing and you need to understand that property investment is a long term investment that can also be hard to liquidate. What this means is simply that you invest in real estate with funds you are willing to keep away for a long time and not funds you will be needing anytime soon - like your emergency funds.

4.   What is a Plot of Land?

A plot is an arbitrary term used to describe a division of land made in a particular area either by the government or the developer, for the purpose of building or farming. It is simply a parcel of land with a demarcation or boundary which is owned or meant to be owned by its owner. In Nigeria today, there are different dimensions; however, a standard plot of land is 60 x 120 Ft. It is generally accepted as 648 square meters, approximately 650 sqm. Some say it is 600 square meters whereas in some areas within Nigeria like Abuja and some areas in the Niger Delta, a plot of land is 450 square meters.

The price for a plot of land varies according to its location. Today, a plot of land in Eko Atlantic costs about $3,000 per square meter which means a plot of 1000sqm will cost about $3,000,000 or thereabout. A plot of land in Magodo, GRA goes for about 80 million per plot while a plot in Ajah axis is averagely about 15-20 million naira.

5.   What is an Acre?

An acre is a standard unit of measurement used by land sellers, it is almost an equivalent to the size of a standard football pitch. An acre is simply 6 plots of land, approximately 4,046sqm. The size of an acre is not the same worldwide; however, the size of an acre can visually be said to be the size of a football pitch.

6.   What is a Hectare?

A hectare is a metric system equivalent to 2.47 acres which consists of 15 plots of land. This is 10,000 square meters, it can be visualized as a rugby field. An acre is about 0.405 of hectare. To simply put it, a hectare is generally accepted to be two and a half acres (2.5 acres) of land.

7.   Who is a Property Investor?

This is someone who actively or passively invests in real estate today with the intention of making bountiful profits in the future. This is a person who indicates interest in and goes ahead to make payment to purchase a property. The property may have been built or still under construction but an investor goes in with a view to enhance it and either resell or lease it out in order to gain a profit. An avid property investor understands the best ways to invest in real estate.

8. Who is a profit grabber in Property Investment?

This is someone who intends creating wealth through real estate investments. Someone who intends to thrive and prosper by taking advantage of opportunities available in the new emerging economy. In some situations, he/ she can also be an early grabber, where he buys into a project or an area at an early stage, anticipating the area or project will boom in a few years, making him have an early taker advantage.

9. What is a Title Document?

A title document is a formal document showing evidence to the ownership of a property - either land or building. In Nigeria, there are some basic title documents that are relevant to landed property ownership, which include the Land Certificate, Certificate of Occupancy, Right of Occupancy, Deed of Assignment, Deed of Lease, Deed of Sublease, Deed of Mortgage, to mention a few.

10.   What is Title?

According to law, a title is a bundle of rights on a piece of property in which a party can either own a legal interest or equitable interest. These rights can be separated or held by different parties. A title is simply the right to own or the ownership of a property.

11.   What is a Title search?

This is a process that examines local public records, laws, ordinances and all related court decisions to determine if any other person has valid claims against the subject property. This is also the confirmation of the authenticity of ownership and status of the subject property. A title search is carried out in due diligence process, ensuring that the person you are negotiating with is the bona fide owner of the property. In some cases, the search also exposes if the owner owes any charges depending on which property it is, where it is located and who developed the property.

12.   What is a Square Meter?

The area of a square that is 1 meter on each side, it is used for measuring spaces, rooms, houses, land etc. A room which is 5 meters on all sides will be 25 square meters.

What is a Corner plot?

A corner plot is located at the intersection of two or more roadways that has frontage on each roadway. A corner plot is slightly bigger and it attracts a significant higher price when compared to a standard or regular plot.

13. What are Land Documents?

These are documents associated with the ownership of land, they are vital papers that anyone who wants to invest in property must know and understand very well; what they mean and the purpose they serve.

14. What is Rental?

This is the possession and not ownership of a property for a specific duration of time which is under defined terms and conditions. While rent is the amount paid for the possession within a specific duration of time, under defined terms and conditions.

15. What is Rental Property?

This is a building which has apartments for rent and not for sale. The owner of this property does not want to sell any part of it but just wants to be receiving rental income which can be paid daily, monthly, quarterly or annually depending on the preference of the owner.

16. Who is a Landlord?

A landlord of a property is simply the owner of the property, or someone acting on behalf of the owner, who must have been given the mandate to operate in such capacity.

17. Who is a Tenant?

A tenant is anyone or any organization who pays a certain amount to the landlord in order to be able to enjoy the access to a facility or building.

18. What is Ownership?

This can be said to be having proprietary right of a land or any piece of real estate which is collectively regarded as the title.

19. What are Amenities?

These are enhancements that buildings offer its owners or its tenants. These usually include children's play room, common lounge, or a gym to mention a few.

20.   What is an Asset?

An asset is something that is owned and has value. Tangible assets such as property, plant and machinery are regarded as fixed assets which cannot be easily converted to cash, while assets such as cash or bank accounts can be described as liquid assets. Property which is real estate is classified as a "real" asset because it has monetary and potential value.

21.   What is Yield as it relates to property?

Yield is the rate of return on an investment which can be land or building. It is usually in percentage (%).

22.   What is a Property Appraisal?

This is an evaluation of a property by a licensed appraiser on its price, based on previous sales of similar properties or other parameters depending on the purpose and use of valuation. In Nigeria, an Estate Surveyor and Valuer is the professional licensed to carry out valuation both for land and buildings and for plant and machinery. Property appraisal also means property valuation, which is the term commonly used in Nigeria.

23. What does Indemnification mean in real estate?

An indemnification clause is a contractual promise by one person or business to reimburse or pay for the monetary losses or damages incurred by another person or business. It is simply the reimbursement or compensation paid to someone for a loss already suffered. So, there can be indemnification in property management agreements, and property leases which also include indemnity clauses.

24. What is an Offer?

An offer is made mostly by the buyer to the seller of a property. An offer letter is an indication of interest to purchase a property at a specific price which can be addressed directly to the seller or seller's representative or agent. When conducting a transaction, it is possible to receive multiple offers during the period while the property is in the market. It is the seller's decision to look through the offers and make a decision on the best offer which sometimes could be the offer with the highest amount.

25. What is an Acceptance letter?

A letter of acceptance is a formal indication of a successful application or offer for a property. This can be written by the individual selling the property or by a real estate agent on your behalf. There are some transactions where acceptance is given verbally; this can be very risky at times. It is advisable to document every step and process in your real estate transaction.

26.   What is a Contract?

This is a legally binding agreement between two parties. In order to have a valid contract of sale in real estate, there must be an offer, an acceptance and payment must have been made and confirmed prior to issuing a contract. A contract is a very detailed document stating clearly the description of the property, size, location, competent parties, legal purpose, and consideration. It must be a written documentation which has the signature of all participants and witnesses.

In simple terms, once an offer is made and accepted, then a contract of sale is issued and signed by the seller acknowledging the receipt of money from the buyer and the buyer must sign also.

27.   What is a Breach of Contract?

It is a legal clause of action in which a binding agreement or bargained-for exchange is not honoured by one or more of the parties to the contract by nonperformance or interference with the other party's performance. It is simply the violation of agreed upon terms and conditions of a binding contract.

28.   What are Building Restrictions?

These are requirements in building code that affect the rise and appearance of a building. These restrictions are mandates giving regulations on what kind of buildings can be developed in a particular area or within an estate. The standard of building materials, building height; the number of floors a building can be and lots more. It is very important to ask and understand the building codes of a particular area before investing in the land. This simple step has cost many individuals and developers a lot of money, energy and time as they could not achieve their expectation because they could not develop the number of floors they had assumed they were going to construct on the land they had bought. This will inevitably affect the projection of the project and can be devastating. Once again, I say, buyers beware.

29.   What is Commission?

In any property transaction, the payment made to a broker or an agent for his or her effort in marketing to buy or to sell or even when managing the property, is called commission. The commission is usually a percentage of the total sale price. Unfortunately, for reasons unknown to me, many people find it difficult to pay for this service and it should not be so. A service that has been provided should be paid for. It is termed professional fees for a reason; every property investor should note that it is mandatory for you to pay commission when you call someone to look for a property for you or help you sell your property. In order words, as a property investor, you must be prepared to pay commission whether you are the one selling or the one buying.

30.   What is a Deed?

This is a written document signed by the seller, which transfers title in one property from one person to another. This can also be referred as the Contract.

31.   What is Encroachment?

This is the act of trespassing on the land of another by a structure or by any other object. It is important that you have the boundaries defined upon purchase. Encroachment or trespassing as it is commonly called is an offence by law; therefore, ensure that you are not encroaching on anybody's land knowingly or unknowingly as ignorance is not an excuse in law. A land surveyor can be called upon to use the survey to define your boundaries clearly to avoid any situation of trespass. I am sure you have seen during road expansion projects that some houses always get pulled down, and for some others, the fence may be completely removed because it was out of their boundaries. The owner must have built on areas marked out for road construction. Once again, I say buyers beware …caveat emptor!

32.   What is Survey?

This is a process of capturing the measurements, boundaries and the area of a property. A survey plan is a document that is produced after this process. It is important I state that a survey plan can be a provisional survey or a registered survey which is quite different so you need to ask which one you are getting especially when you are being lured to pay for survey by property developers. Be guided!

33.   What is Encumbrance?

This is simply a claim or a liability attached to a property. It is a very powerful word; I use the word powerful because it is important that you are investing in a property that is free from government encumbrance. Should the land or property not be stated "Free from Government Encumbrance", the risk is quite high except you are aware while buying into it. A clear example of this is land with the "Excision in process" tag.

34.   What is Zoning?

A zone is an area of a city or specific building that is mapped out "zoned" for a specific use, such as the residential area, industrial area, and the Central Business Districts (CBD). Zoning are laws regulating the land use of a particular area, so it is important to pay attention to the zoning laws of the area you are investing in.

35.   What is Useful life of a property?

This is simply the period of time in which a property is expected to be economically useful. The phrase of import here is" economically useful", which is very paramount when you are investing in distressed properties. Some property developers are interested in buying and restructuring distressed buildings without conducting an integrity test on such buildings after purchase and this can be very dangerous. Many times, these properties are resold to unsuspecting investors after giving them a cosmetic uplift for a profit margin or some are given out to tenants for rent or sometimes, it can even possibly be a joint venture they had with the initial owners. Therefore, as an investor, it is important for you to ask questions concerning the history of the property you are buying before parting with your hard earned money.

36.   What is Property Obsolescence?

Obsolescence is another word for depreciation which arises due to physical deterioration or normal wear and tear. Obsolescence occurs generally due to the availability of alternatives that perform better or are cheaper or both. It may also be due to the changes in the user preferences/requirement.

In most cases, when a building is obsolete and being bought by a property investor probably due to interest in the location, it is advisable to demolish and regenerate the property to suit today's market, especially if the intention is to resell or rent it out for rental income. It is also important I clarify that it is only the building that depreciates as land does not depreciate.

37.   What is Joint venture?

This is a business arrangement in which two or more parties agree to pool their resources together for the purpose of accomplishing a specific task. For instance, the owner of a land may be approached by someone who has resources to build, and they agree and draw up a written contract on what kind of property they intend building and also agree on the sharing formula of the property upon completion. Another important decision that is considered during a joint venture agreement is the duration of time/holding period that the developer has to use the property for profit before returning it to the initial owners. Another consideration is an amount of money known as "premium" to be paid. This premium must also be discussed and agreed upon by all parties involved, which is largely dependent on the type and preference of joint venture that is being done. It is also important that when deciding to do a joint venture, the integrity of the other parties involved as well as their financial capacity must be considered. This is because you do not want to do business with a company that would not be able to complete and deliver the project due to financial constraints.

38.   What is "CAVEAT EMPTOR?"

This is a legal term that simply means "buyers beware". Yes, buyers beware because really, it is the buyer that is about to part with valuable "hard earned money".

As a property investor, it is important to ask questions; no question is irrelevant. The purpose of creating this book is to give you insights on what you should know, and shed light on areas that might have not been clear to you in the past, **Knowledge they say is Power.** It is important that you are equipped with the right knowledge as you begin to invest in property, especially in Nigeria. Whenever you are in doubt, you need to seek professional help. As you go further into reading this book, you will be learning about some of the professionals in the real estate industry. It is important you know who they are, what they do and what institutions they belong to. I believe this will serve as a guide.

2

GETTING TO KNOW YOUR PROFESSIONALS

39. Who are the major professionals in landed matters?

Some professionals that participate in the real estate industry include:

- *Estate surveyor and valuer*
- *Lawyer*
- *Architect*
- *Land surveyor*
- *Quantity surveyor*
- *Builder*
- *Town planner*
- *Structural engineer*

40. Who is an Estate Surveyor and Valuer?

An Estate Surveyor and Valuer is a professional trained in the art and science of Estate Management to direct and supervise an interest in landed properties, with the sole aim of obtaining optimum returns for the owners of such properties. An Estate Surveyor and Valuer are also referred as "land economists" those who are qualified and licensed belongs to the Nigerian Institution of Estate Surveyors and Valuers (NIESV).

41. Who is a Land Surveyor?

This is a professional who is trained in the science of determining the terrestrial or three-dimensional positions of points and the distance and angles between them. A registered land surveyor who is qualified belongs to the Nigerian Institution of Surveyors (NIS).

42. Who is a Lawyer?

A lawyer is a generic term used to describe anyone who is a licensed legal practitioner qualified to give legal advice in one or more areas of law. In Nigeria, a lawyer belongs to the Nigerian Bar Association (NBA). The lawyer can be involved in the negotiation of the property and they prepare the deed on your behalf.

43. Who is an Architect?

An architect is a professional who plans, designs and reviews the construction of buildings. An architect produces the architectural drawings; the plan and model of the building or project. In Nigeria today, a certified architect belongs to the Nigerian Institution of Architects (NIA).

44.   Who is a Quantity Surveyor?

A registered quantity surveyor is a professional who calculates the costing, that is, the amount of materials needed for building work, and how much they will charge. In Nigeria today, a Quantity Surveyor who is qualified belongs to the Nigerian Institution of Quantity Surveyors (NIQS).

45.   What is Quantity Surveying and how can it help property investors?

Quantity surveying is a highly specialized field involved in estimating and monitoring construction costs. Quantity surveyors specialize in building measurement and estimating the value costs to ascertain the value of building work, including new construction, refurbishment additions and renovations.

46.   Who is a Builder?

Builders oversee and undertake a range of projects in the construction industry. The Nigerian Institute of Building is the professional body of Builders and those that are engaged in the building profession.

47. Who is a Town Planner?

A town planner's responsibility is to ease or avoid social, economic and environmental problems within the town. They are also in charge of designing and creating estate layouts in order to have a functional estate or community. A registered town planner belongs to the Nigerian Institution of Town Planners (NITP).

48. Who is a Structural Engineer?

A structural engineer is a professional who is involved in the designing of structures such as buildings, bridges, tunnels. Majority of structural engineers work hand in hand with architects or building-design contractors as consultants. Council for the Regulation of Engineering in Nigeria- COREN is the governing body for engineers.

49. What are Professional fees?

Professional fees are money paid to professionals for utilizing their expertise in a transaction. It includes the agency fee paid to the estate surveyor and valuer as well as the legal fees paid to the lawyer for every property transaction as the case may be. It is very important you include these fees when creating an estimate or budget for the purchase or sale of your property.

50.   How best can I negotiate professional fees?

The best way to negotiate professional fees is by dialogue and it is meant to be discussed at the beginning of the transaction. There must be an agreed rate to be paid which must be acceptable to all parties involved. You do not just offer any figure you feel like at the end of the transaction, it is very wrong.

Please note, the reasons the institutions were mentioned above is because they are backed up by the Nigerian Constitution, so when you are dealing with ANY of these professionals you should be rest assured ideally, as they have ethics guarding their profession , they also have membership numbers.

As a buyer or an investor, when you use qualified professionals in your business transactions, the advantages cannot be overemphasized, they can never run away with your money, they are traceable and can be reported for professional misconduct, professional negligence or malpractice to their institutions in a case where you are dissatisfied with the service and unable to resolve them. There are a lot of people who have the wrong perception and go ahead to patronize quacks instead, they end up paying the price when they get their fingers burnt and learn the hard way. Using professionals in all your property transactions saves you money, energy and time.

3

UNDERSTANDING LAND CLASSIFICATION AND STATUS OF LAND

In this section of the book, you will be learning about the general overview of land ownership in simple terms, understanding that land in some areas in Nigeria still have the Freehold especially for owners before the coming of the Land Use Act. You will learn the difference between the federal and state Certificate of Occupancy. You will also be learning about the Land Use Act of 1978, what it means, what brought about it, who established the act and the different status that land can have here in Nigeria. This section is highly educative and should be interesting to you as you read.

51.   What does the term "Land classification" mean?

Land can be classified as either free or acquired. A parcel of land is considered free if the government has not indicated any interest whatsoever in that land.

Such land is safe to buy because the title on the land can be perfected without issues. In most cases, such lands will either have a gazette, a C of O or a Governor's consent.

52.   What are the types of classification? There are two types of acquisition:
- Committed Acquisition
- Global / General Acquisition

Committed Acquisition: A parcel of land is said to be under committed acquisition when the government has indicated an intention to use that land for a specific purpose such as provision of amenities.

Such lands belong to the government and cannot be available for use by individuals. If you purchase land that is under committed acquisition, it will be impossible for you to perfect your land title and you will only be occupying the land illegally until the government comes to kick you out without any compensation. You end up losing time, money and all, therefore, Committed lands are such that have been set apart clearly for use, which can be for future road expansion, bridges, universities, community hospitals, cemeteries, housing projects and other projects the government deems fit.

The point here is that as an investor, it is important to verify the area you are buying before you pay to acquire any land or building. For example, areas in Lagos where the upcoming 4th mainland bridge would pass through have been mapped out in the Master plan. It is there, so if you refuse to do your independent checks and you buy such land either as an individual investor or even as a developer, then there is fire on the mountain. You need to run from such investments as they would ultimately go bad and that is money down the drain. Once again, I say to you– buyers beware!

53.   What do you understand by Global or General Acquisition?

Land that is under "general acquisition" or "global acquisition" is actually acquired by the government of the state but there is *no specific purpose* yet for keeping the land. Sometimes, it is possible that the government can release such land for private use then it can be said to be *'free'* or when the government decides to be specific about what they want to do with the land then it becomes *'committed'* as the case may be. A land under general acquisition can become free by a process called excision.

54.   What is the Land Use Act?

Before now, the traditional families have so much power when it comes to anything regarding land, they determine which land is to be sold or kept for future use. These families had very strong power over land and many of them refused to sell to those who needed it, making it difficult for anyone who wants to buy land for industries, schools and other social benefits. There were also lots of tussles over land especially in areas where natural resources were found. Based on this and several other reasons, the government under the administration of General Olusegun Obasanjo led the proclamation of the **Land Use Decree 1978;** vested *all lands into the hands of the government* and the governor of each state became the administrator.

The Land Use Act coupled with other laws empowered the governor to acquire more lands compulsorily for its own public purpose to provide for the greater good of the citizens.

The government still recognizes that the indigenes of the community have a right to their land, hence it is customary for the state government to release a portion of their land back to the original owners when there is a need for it.

For every land in Nigeria, below are the possible status a land can possess:

- Acquired land
- Committed land
- Rectifiable land
- Excised land
- Free land

55.   What is Acquired Land?

An acquired land is land which belongs to the government. However, in some cases, such a land may be released to the village, where the portion released and the purpose of the release would be sated. The probability of getting an acquired land released back to the villagers is quite slim. *Here again, we see excision which would be explained as we go further…*

56.   What is Committed Land?

A committed land is land strictly belonging to the government. The land has been specifically committed for projects. You are not meant to buy committed land as it is a very high risk. Unsuspecting buyers and investors end up paying for such land and they get duped losing their hard earned money.

57.   What is Excision?

Excision is the first stage of perfecting a title for an acquired land, it actually means a portion of land has been *legally released* to indigenous settlers (villagers) by state or federal government. Thus, such portion of land is legally free from government acquisition.

Excision simply means taking out a part from a whole initially committed sum of land Making that *the released part to* be the *Excised Land*; meaning it is free and can be bought for private use. This will afterwards be recorded and documented in the gazette of that state.

In other words, if a parcel of land that was formerly under acquisition becomes excised: it is then considered free and it is now an excised land.

What is Excision in progress? This is simply the process whereby the villages (indigenes/families) are requesting that government releases a portion of their acquired land to them legally. Excision can only be released to a village and not a developer, that is why it is called a Village Excision and most times it is released to them on social benefit grounds/claims.

58.   What is a Gazette?

A gazette is an official record book where all special government details are spelt out, detailed and recorded. A gazette will show the communities or villages that have been granted excision and the number of acres or hectares of land that the government has given to them.

It is within those excised acres or hectares that the traditional family is entitled to sell its lands to the public and not anything outside those hectares of land given or excised to them.

If they decide to sell anything outside the excised land, it is a danger zone to anyone who buys it as they (the family and their buyers) have trespassed by selling a portion of land that has passed their boundaries. This means that a portion of land under acquisition by the government has been sold to unsuspecting investors. Once again, I say "Buyers Beware!" Always do your independent checks before parting with your money. It is when your money is still in your pocket you have all the power, once you part with your money, it is time to call 911. You start litigation which will cost you energy, time and money; let's not even mention the psychological trauma, the stress and risk to your health.

Here are some more details you will find handy as well about the Gazette. The cover of the gazette must include the number, pages and volume of the gazette. It must also include the location and date it was issued.

• The first page of a gazette must have the following unless it is a dubious or fake gazette:
o The logo of the state and the inscription of the title "Lagos State of Nigeria Official Gazette"
o Underneath, it must have the number, volume, page, date and the location it was signed into law. For example, you will see something like this written on it; No 29 in pages 205 to 291, Volume 84 dated 30th of April 2011 *(by the way, the numbers in this example are not real numbers to any legal document, they are just for the purpose of learning an example of how the numbers will look)* and have the content of the list of the villages, settlements and parcels of land excised back to the community.

The inner pages will show the following:
- The description of the area or village excised
- The number of acres or hectares of land excised to the village.
- Where the boundaries of the beacons start and stop.

59.   What is free land?

This is simply a portion of land that is free from government acquisition. These are land that you can buy and be assured peace of mind without having any fear that the government will take over ownership. Although, it is important I state clearly that being a free land does not mean it cannot be used or obtained by the government, it only means when such happens, you will be compensated.

4

Understanding your Land Documents

I believe you are having a good time reading this book, I want to also believe you find it very enlightening and an easy read as that was the purpose of writing it in the first place. I find it very interesting every time I pick it up. As you proceed, you will be learning more about the papers now. What are they, who prepares them, why you need to have them, who can help you with getting your documents and all. Knowing and understanding land documents is essential in your real estate journey as an investor. Keep reading, I hope you find it valuable.

60. What is a Survey Plan?

This is one of the most important documents you must ask for. Most especially for those that are buying from the *'omo-onile'*. Why? You may ask. This is because it shows the measurement of the boundary. It gives an accurate measurement and description of the land which is handled by a land surveyor and regulated by the office of the surveyor general of each state.

In simple terms, a survey plan is a document that measures the boundary of a parcel of land to give an accurate measurement and description of that land. The people that handle survey issues are land surveyors. For example, in Lagos, all survey matters, issuing, and regulations are handled by the office of the Surveyor General in Alausa. A typical survey plan must contain the following information:

- *The name of the owner of the land surveyed.*
- *The address or description of the land surveyed.*
- *The size of the land surveyed.*
- *The drawn out portion of the land surveyed and mapped out on the survey plan document.*
- *The beacon numbers.*
- *The surveyor who drew up the survey plan and the date it was drawn up.*

61.   What is a Deed of Conveyance?

Deed of Conveyance or Registered Conveyance was the authentic evidence of ownership until 1978 Land Use Act that introduced Certificate of Occupancy.

Deed of Conveyance is the old legal document used in transferring the interest of the owner of a landed property to another whom it is assigned, the assignee. When ownership is transferred, the new legal document which is in use now is called Deed of

Assignment. There are quite a lot of properties which have a Deed of Conveyance as their title, which is actually valid. You will find more of houses with deed of conveyance in areas like Surulere, Yaba, and Ebute Metta especially.

62.   What is a Deed of Assignment?

This is the agreement between the seller of the land and the buyer showing the evidence that the seller has transferred all his rights, title, interest and ownership of the land to the buyer.

Most people have the title documents to their cars intact and in safe places but fail to ask for the Deed of Assignment to their properties which is several times more valuable than cars. It amazes me when I hear people say that they do not have a deed of assignment, forgetting that it is one vital land document that shows that a buyer is now the new owner of a land/ property.

A Deed of Assignment is one of the transactional documents drawn up by a real estate attorney between the former title holder for a particular property and the new buyer.

When ownership is transferred, the Deed of Assignment shows the new legal owner of the property. The deed contains very pertinent information for a real estate transaction. It spells out the date when the ownership of the property transfers from one owner to the other. The deed also states clearly a specific description of the property whose interest is being transferred. **It is very compulsory and mandatory for a Deed of Assignment document to be recorded at the appropriate land registry to show legal evidence as to the exchange of ownership in any land/landed property transaction as the case may be in order to make the general public and government aware of such exchange or transaction.**

In simple terms, in every real estate transaction today, a Deed of Assignment is a legal document that transfers the interest of the owner to the person to whom it is assigned, the assignee. The new owner must do a change of ownership, hence perfect the title to the ownership of the new acquired property. The importance to the Perfection of Title cannot be over emphasized.

63.   What is a Certificate of Occupancy?

A Certificate of Occupancy (C of O) is a land document issued by the government to officially lease land to you, the applicant, for 99 years. As already discussed above, according to the land use act of 1978, all lands belong to the government. A certificate of occupancy is, however, the officially recognized land document for demonstrating exclusive right to a land. The C of O as it is popularly called also indicates that the structures of any improvements made to these structures comply with the codes, ordinances and regulations of that government entity and they can be occupied. It is important that I state clearly that there **cannot** be two (2) Certificates on a particular land/property. This means that if a land has a Certificate of Occupancy, another one cannot be issued on that land anymore even for the future buyers.

There are 4 types of Certificates of Occupancy which are Individual, Global, Company and Scheme

- The individual C of O is the certificate issued to an individual so it will be in the name of that person. For example, Mojisola Afolayan.
- A global Certificate of Occupancy can be for a town or a community or an estate. For instance, Ogombo Certificate of Occupancy.
- A company Certificate of Occupancy will be written in the name of the company that acquired the property. For instance, MAE Limited.

- The scheme Certificate of Occupancy will be for a government scheme like the Lekki Scheme 2 Certificate of Occupancy or the Abijo GRA scheme.

64. What does the term "Governor's' Consent" mean?

Since there cannot be two Certificates of Occupancy on a particular property, if the owner of an existing land having a C of O decides to sell his land, the only documents that can be given to the new buyer or subsequent buyers is a Governor's Consent. A Governor's Consent can only be processed on a land which already has either Gazette or an Existing Certificate of Occupancy (C of O).

The powers of the Governor to consent to such transactions can be found in Section 22 of the Land Use Act of 1978 which states thus "It shall not be lawful for the holder of a statutory right of occupancy granted by the governor to alienate his right of occupancy or any part thereof by assignment, mortgage, transfer of possession, sublease or otherwise howsoever without the consent of the Governor first hand and obtained." This simply means therefore that even when a buyer has secured a land with a Certificate of Occupancy, he shouldn't stop there. He needs to begin the process of obtaining a Governor's consent to make that purchase legal in the eyes of the government and rest assured his land is safe. An advantage of having a Governor's Consent is that you can also transfer your rights on a land to another person without going back to the 'omo-onile' or the 'Baales' of the community to sign your Deed and Form 1C which are compulsory requirements before you can process Governor's Consent.

65.   What does the term "Deed of Mortgage" mean?

This is a legal document that gives the mortgagee (lender of a loan) an interest in a property. If the mortgagor (borrower who takes loan) does not pay back the loan as agreed in the contract, the lender can foreclose and take possession of the land or even have it auctioned.

In a mortgage transaction, the mortgagor is the borrower who obtains loan from the lender and pledges his property as a security for repayment. Mortgagee is the lender who gives the loan to the mortgagor and receives the security interest in the property.

66.   What does the term "Deed of Partitioning" mean?

This a deed by which lands or property held in common, or joint tenancy are separated into different portions and distributed among the people involved. This simply means the deed is used to divide a property among different people who are usually family members. A partition is a division of a property held jointly with several persons so that each person has the right and becomes the owner of the share allocated to him or her.

67.   What does the term "Federal Certificate of Occupancy" mean?

This is the title document given to an individual, company or organization for a 99-year lease granted by the Federal Government for lands belonging to the Federal Government. Please note that you cannot change a Federal Certificate of Occupancy to a State Certificate of Occupancy. There are some plots in Ikoyi that their title is Federal Certificate of Occupancy and all enquires on such properties will be directed to the Federal Ministry of Lands and not the State. Interestingly, there are Federal Lands in all the 36 states of the federation and there are Federal Ministry of Land offices in every state as well so it is important for you as an investor to ask questions so you know the office governing your property investment.

68. What does the term "Minister's Consent" mean? This is a secondary transaction you get after a title document called the Federal C of O as the rooting title. Just as you have Governor's consent for lands being sold after a state Certificate of Occupancy, you have the Minister's consent for Federal Certificate of Occupancy. This means that anywhere you have Federal Government land, you have a Minister's Consent which can be in any of the 36 states in Nigeria. Note there is Federal Government land in all the 36 states in Nigeria and not only in the FCT, Abuja.

69. **What is a Land Certificate?**
This is a document of title as to the ownership of a piece or large parcel of land issued by a government's land registry for registered freehold or leasehold lands in Nigeria prior to the promulgation of the Land Use Act of 1978. Land Certificate was usually issued to owners of land and landed properties when the Property Conveyancing Law of 1959 was still in effect. It refers to the Prima facie evidence of land

ownership prior to the promulgation of the Land Use Act which vests on lands in the governor of each state of the federation.

70. What does the term "Contract of sale" mean?

A contract of sale or sale's contract, is a document indicating the purchase of a property.

Please Note: A CONTRACT OF SALE is NOT a title document

71. What is Offer letter?

This is the letter that expresses the intention of a buyer to purchase a property. If you get an offer letter and you do not go ahead to make payment, you don't have any property. This letter most times carries all the details of the transaction such as the terms and conditions, mode of payment, period, payment details etc.

Please note: An Offer letter is NOT a title document and not a legally binding Contract.

72. What is Letter of Allocation?

This shows a land or property has been allocated to you. Both federal and state government also issue a letter of allocation, it may be for site and service where they state the type and structure you are to build on the land. There can also be payment plan in form of a mortgage where payment is made in instalments from your salary. You can also make outright payment and get a final allocation letter after all payments have been made. It is still important for you to perfect your title whether you bought from government or from individuals or private developers.

Please Note: An Allocation Letter Is NOT A Title Document.

73.   What does the term "Receipts" mean in a real estate transaction?

A lot of times, many people confuse a receipt and a deed of assignment. No, it is not the same thing. A payment receipt is the least of all in the hierarchy of land documents globally. I say this because it does not have any legal weight per se, it is just an acknowledgement given by the seller to the buyer indicating that he / she has received money in exchange for his land without any form of compulsion. A receipt is simply an evidence of transaction.

Please Note: A Receipt Is NOT A Title Document.

5

Other "Nagging" Everyday Questions

In this section, you will be learning from previously asked questions, which are quite relatable as they are general everyday questions that require clarity. I used the word "everyday" because people tend to seek clarifications on some of these questions over and over again. Do read, enjoy and more importantly, I hope you learn from the book as it will serve as a guide when you are investing in your next property.

74. What is the responsibility of a lawyer in landed matters?

The lawyer is a professional required to perfect the title of the land. The lawyer is also required to conduct search and authenticity of legal /title documents for all sorts of landed transactions. As a buyer or an investor, it is important you contact your lawyer to prepare the deed of assignment you will be giving to the seller to sign.

75. Why do I need the services of an estate surveyor and valuer when buying property?

This real estate professional should be your first point of call once you are ready to start investing in properties. He will advise you on the best available options, he/she will also ensure you get the best deal and most importantly, ensure the transaction is in your best interest.

76. What is the difference between ownership and possession?

When it comes to real estate, ownership is totally different from possession. Possession is the moment when you have complete access to the apartment you just bought or the land you just paid for while ownership is the moment you have made payment and have the appropriate title documents. This means you have perfected your title in your name. Please note, if you have any property and you have not yet perfected your title, you have only possessed the property, there is no ownership yet. Unfortunately, many people, young and old, literates or not are on this table, they have not perfected their title after so many years either as a result of ignorance or lack of money as at the time of purchase. It is important to keep this in mind and **TREAT AS PRIORITY**.

Another problem arises when the person dies interstate, it becomes very difficult for the children to lay claim to the property. **Remember, no title, no ownership... It is that simple.**

77. How can I take possession over my land when I am not ready to build at the moment?

As simple as this sounds, a lot of people have lost their investment because they did not know what to do. The simplest way to take possession over a land even when you are not ready to build; especially for an 'omo-onile' land is to build a fence around the land and put a gate. In a situation where you cannot fence it, ensure you create your presence on such land by pouring truckloads of granite, blocks or even you can be using the land for farming purposes. It is advisable for you not to leave your land empty, by all means ensure you take possession so you do not lose your land.

78. Can I just leave my land in trust to the 'omo-onile' to watch over for me?

No, you must never completely entrust the possession or security of your land into any one's hands, not neighbours, not friends or family members to watch over. Never leave your land void. It is very risky and should by all means be avoided.

79.   What is 'omo-onile' land?

This is a Yoruba word describing land belonging to the indigenous land owners, 'Omo-onile' are the legitimate owners of land under customary law. However, in today's world, there is a general link of the word 'omo-onile' to violence as these people are known for their notorious act even after buyers pay for a land. They are generally referred to as 'land grabbers' because they can sell one plot to two or more persons thus leading to confusion.

80.   How best can I buy an 'omo-onile' land?

Depending on your preference and current conditions, buying the 'Omo-Onile' land might be the best option for you with a caveat of you understanding the dos and don'ts.

If you seek professional help, you should be able to buy any land without hassles. **Essentially, having a professional to guide you step by step is the right guide advised if you must invest in 'Omo-onile' land, especially in areas that are just developing.**

81.   Can I give my land to neighbours to farm?

Many times, giving land to neighbours within an area to farm is seen as a safe method of securing your land and avoiding the land from laying fallow so it does not seem abandoned. However, owner's discretion is advised. *You need to thread that path with caution when considering this option.*

82.   Can I give my land to mechanics / religious houses to use pending the time I am ready to build?

There is a myth around this claim, giving your vacant plot to mechanics for free pending the time to build is generally perceived as a safe method of securing your land; however, it has its down side. Professionally, it is not advisable because you might find it difficult evicting them when you are ready to put your land to use or even sell at a future date. All the same, owner's discretion is advised.

83.   What is the value of a land?

Land value is the economic worth of a land. It is simply the measure of how much the piece of real estate is worth. Many times, this does not include the building or other improvements that might be on the land at that time. Land value is generally associated with a vacant plot but it can also be the cost of an undeveloped land or a built property.

84.   What is the Difference between Land Price and Land Value?

The property price is the amount that you can pay for a property at a particular time, this can be simply described as how much you paid or are willing to pay for a property versus how much the property is really worth in the market, which is the value. This is largely dependent on the economy, the buying power of an individual which ideally is a reflection of how the economy of the country is responding to inflation, as well as the demand and supply

85.   What is the Market value of a property?

This is an opinion of the best price at which a property /asset would be sold in a competitive market under all conditions requisite to a fair sale with the buyer and the seller each acting prudently, knowledgeably and assuming price is not affected by undue stimulus. It can be explained as the worth of a property in the market as at today. Market value is dependent on the structural attributes, land rates, land use and location of the property.

86.   What does Forced Sale Value mean?

This is the estimate of the amount that a seller would agree to sell his property under harsh "desperate" conditions (which are mostly unforeseen or uncontrollable conditions). This is usually about 70% of the market value.

87.   What does "Fair Market Value" mean?

The *fair market value* of a property is the estimated price to which a knowledgeable, interested buyer and a seller would agree. It is important that we understand the term *"fair market value"* is just an estimate, and the actual price the land eventually sells may be higher or lower than the market value.

88.   Depreciated replacement cost: This is the cost of acquiring an equally satisfactory substitute asset. Peradventure there is an accident, the amount will it cost to replace or rebuild another property of good quality similar to that which was damaged or destroyed is the depreciated replacement cost.

89.   How many plots make an acre?

An acre consists of 6 plots

90.   How many plots make a hectare?

A hectare consists of 15 plots.

For example if a client wants to purchase 3 hectares of land for development, what she wants is simply 15 x 3 = 45 plots of land

91.   Should I buy land within an estate?

This is mainly an investor's decision which is based on your preference /choice. It is the buyer's decision based on his current preference and situation. Most estates are gated communities with provisions such as having 24 hours security, tarred roads, street lights, designated public areas, play areas, private areas, shopping area, swimming pool, sports complex to mention a few .

92.   Why do I need to pay more money after paying for the land?

All around the world, there are other levies and charges that accompany the price of the land when purchased - such as documentation fee, development fees and service provision fees.

93.   What are the additional fees for?

These are fees you pay to ensure you get the highest and best (optimum value) from your property or land as the case maybe. These additional fees also foster the provision and maintenance of amenities, you were promised at the time of purchase.

94. What are development fees?

These are money paid to a development company for the provision of facilities which include roads, street lights, swimming pool and also to maintain the estate; especially in undeveloped areas / estates. In most cases, payment of development fee is meant to be a one-off payment. For some estates, the payment must be made before getting possession over that land or building you have just purchased.

95. What is service charge?

When you acquire a property that has services provided, you will be levied to pay service charge. This can be described as a maintenance levy paid for the provision of services provided in the vicinity where your property is located. In most cases, these charges cover security levy, provision of electricity and water, cleaning of common areas, maintenance of swimming pool, generator and lots more. Please note: Service charge are regular payments which can be paid annually, monthly or quarterly depending on the developer and/or the occupants of the premises.

96.   What does documentation fees mean?

This is the money you pay for your documentation especially when dealing with a development company. Such fees include survey fees, the legal fees for the deed that would be prepared, and other title documents depending on the type and location of the property you have just acquired.

97.   Can I pay cash for my land or property?

As a real estate professional, I advise you do not pay cash for any property. No matter the pressure or circumstance, ensure you use bank instruments such as cheques, bank transfer, bank drafts etc. for all payments pertaining to your real estate investment.

98.   Must I sign agreements or contracts when I purchase my property?

Yes, it is very important you sign contracts as you are exchanging ownership of title over the land/property. It must be documented legally while you take possession.

99.   Who is the best person to prepare the agreement?

The buyer's attorney is best advised to prepare the deed. The reason for this is to ensure that the details of the deed is in the buyer's interest and not otherwise.

100. Can the seller arrange for the agreement to be prepared?

In some cases, especially when buying from a development company, they usually prepare the deed. However, if the buyer is not comfortable with the arrangement, the buyer should make a request, but if the buyer is uncomfortable with the process, then he / she can look for an alternative property or they both agree on a mutually beneficial term between the buyer and seller.

101. When is the best time to buy land?

The best time to buy land is now. Give no room for procrastination. Take that bold step and get into action the right way.

102. When do I have to make payment for a property I am about to acquire?

When all due diligence processes have been carried out and you are sure that the person (s) you are dealing with is genuine as well as the land / property you are about to own is valid.

103.   Should I transfer all the money at once?

It is advisable to split the entire money to be paid. The money can be paid twice or three times and should there be any funny occurrence, you would still have some money with you.

104.   What do I need to do before paying for the land?

You need to ensure due diligence, ensure you are dealing with credible people, if it is a company, you need to know the people behind the brand and whenever you are in doubt, you should seek professional help.

105.   What does due diligence mean?

In property acquisition, due diligence is an investigation process, it is simply taking reasonable steps before parting with funds to avoid making any mistake.

Why do I need to do due diligence?

Conducting a search before investing is paramount. Due diligence is carried out to avoid losing your hard earned money to fraudsters.

106. How do I do due diligence before buying 'Omo-onile' land?

Get a surveyor to confirm to you the co-ordinates and status of the property you intend buying, get your lawyer to conduct necessary checks at the land registry, and talk to an estate surveyor to guide you through the property acquisition process when you are in doubt.

107. How do I do due diligence when buying property from a developer?

Make research on the company; who is behind the brand, what projects have they handled before, what are people saying about them, the houses they have built before, etc. Make sure you visit the place and ask questions and whenever you are in doubt, seek professional help.

108. Why do I need to do Independent checks?

It is important you conduct your independent checks so you are not making decisions on what a seller told you. You need to beware of fraudsters and not lose your money. If it sounds too good to be true, it probably is too good to be true. Caveat Emptor!

109.   What papers do I need to conduct document authenticity search?

This is based on the type of property you intend acquiring and the location. In Nigeria generally, you can have a survey, the Certificate of Occupancy, the deed to mention a few.

110.   Do I need to cite the original land documents?

Yes, it is highly advisable to cite the original documents and ensure you collect same from the seller after purchase as they no longer belong to the seller. Keep all original documents in a safe and secure place. Ensure no compromise, no assumptions, no damage, and no theft.

111.   Can I use copies of the document for the search?

Yes, just ensure you see the original documents before parting with your money and ensure you collect the originals immediately after the transfer of funds as they now belong to you.

112. If the seller refuses to release the copies of the document after negotiation, can I use just the volume and page number for the search?

From my experience- More often than not, this seems to be a red flag.

113. Why do I need to do Independent survey?

To be double sure that the co-ordinates stated in the survey plan handed to you by the seller is actually the same as the co-ordinates of the land you just purchased. A Land surveyor is who you need to help you with that.

114. When can I get allocation for the land I just bought?

Allocation can be linked to possession and it should be immediate once full payment has been made.

115. Why do I have to wait for months before I can get allocation?

Many development companies selling land or property within estates claim they prefer physical allocation is done as a group especially for areas that are just developing. This also gives them time to complete the intending construction work on site. As a buyer, you need to follow up and ask questions.

116.   Must I do a full fence all at once since I want to take possession?

When it comes to taking possession, it is advisable to erect a fence on your newly acquired plot of land. However, if you feel you want to commence building straight away instead of committing funds to erecting fence you can also do as long as it indicates you are on your land that you have paid for. So, whether you are ready to build or not, it is a good idea. You also need to check the rules and regulation about how far back the fence needs to be set on your property; sometimes, this is about 4 to 6 inches from the property line but it is important to check with the laws of the area your property is located. If it is within an estate, you may have to check with the association as they may also have rules about fence placement, the height and the material to be used for constructing the fence.

117.   What are the costs associated to property?
Property costs can be described in 4 ways:

- The cost of the property itself: this is the actual price paid initially to acquire the land or building.
- The cost for documentation: this is the payment made in ensuring that you do the

transfer of rights correctly and legally. It can include the signing of documents, and survey.

- The cost for infrastructure: this is the payment incurred as development levy.
- The cost for maintenance: this sometimes is paid as service charge.

118.   What does Home Equity mean?

Home equity is simply the portion of your property that you truly own. You are certainly considered to own your own home, but if you borrowed money to buy it, like getting a mortgage, your lender also has interest in the property until you pay off the loan completely.

119.   What are wetlands and dry lands?

Wetlands are areas inundated by water either temporarily or permanently. Wet lands occur where water meets land and they take many forms including marshes, swamps, mangroves, lagoons, lakes and floodplains. In Lagos for example, there are areas which are associated with wet land areas like some parts of Ebute-Metta, Magodo, Gbagada and Lekki axis so it is always recommended to do a proper research and analysis before going ahead to construct on wetlands or you go and build elsewhere if possible. Many construction projects have failed to do the right thing and go through the ideal process because they cut corners as they went ahead to build in areas prone to wetness without caution. If you are to build on wetlands, permits are usually required in many places, also the cost of construction on wetlands are usually higher, they far exceed pre and construction costs especially for the salt water wetlands when compared to fresh water wetlands.

Let me tell you a short story about a colleague of mine who had a choice of buying a plot of dry land in Ogba, an area in Lagos but saw a cheaper plot which was a waterlogged plot, all because it was cheaper and also easily accessible to the express road and that is why many people make wrong investment decisions all because they didn't seek professional help. This colleague of mine started to develop his site and later realized the cost of sand filling would have taken him far in the building itself if he had bought the dry land. This story is synonymous to what many Lagosians encounter from time to time because Lagos is an island and many parts are wetlands.

If you must build on a waterlogged or marshy land, you must be ready to sand fill the land, let it settle, and concrete must be used on the lower part of the foundation as well as the fence above the proper floor level. The foundation must be high and above the road level.

120.   Dry land?

This is the opposite of wetlands, they are areas identified with scarcity of water.

121.   What kind of foundation do I need to do on the island?

Most times, a raft foundation or pile foundation is advised depending on the number of floors you want to build.

122.   How much does it cost to do a foundation?

It depends on the location of your land and the type of foundation required. A structural engineer can provide more details on this.

123.   How and when can I sell my land?

It depends on the reason you bought the land in the first place, have the land ready with all its documents, fix a price you want to sell and know the type of buyer you would target that would be interested in buying. It is also important that you are aware of the current market value and you work with an estate surveyor and valuer to guide your decisions.

124. Are there mortgage opportunities available in Nigeria?

Yes, there are mortgage opportunities in Nigeria, you only need to be credit worthy and more importantly, you must be able to make your required down payment of about 20-30% minimum contribution and the balance is spread over a number of years.

125. If I want to invest in land today, are there flexible payment plans?

Yes, there are estates which are sites and serviced estates that offer flexible payment plan from three months up to twelve months, depending on the terms and conditions of the development company selling.

126. What does Rent-to-Own mean?

This is a property owning strategy where you pay rent on a property with the end goal being ownership of the property.

127. Is the Certificate of Occupancy the only title recognized by law in Nigeria?

No, it is not, there are several other valid land title documents.

128.   If I buy a property that has a Certificate of Occupancy, can I also get my own Certificate of Occupancy?

No, you cannot get another Certificate of Occupancy, as it can only be issued once to a particular land or property, and cannot be issued twice.

129.   Now that I cannot get a Certificate of Occupancy, what do I get?

In a situation where you cannot get a Certificate of Occupancy, you get a Governor's Consent.

130. As an investor who is new in town how and where do you advice I meet my agents?

Either you are a new investor or an experienced investor or even if you are a realtor I will advise that you always schedule the first meetings at your own office. I will also add that you make sure someone knows where, when and with whom you are going for inspections. This is another valuable reason why investors should have a real estate professional involved in your transactions. Don't be too secretive with your investments move, been too secretive can also be a red flag when it comes to investment

As agents, I will advise you also are very careful, do not jump into cars of clients you do not know well and when you find that you have to be alone, ensure you stay in contact with someone from your office, family or home.

When it comes to real estate investing your safety can not be over emphasized, as much as you can ensure upon entry into a property you identify the exits and you generally avoid scary or impromptu meetings or inspections, I know we want to seal that deal but caution is KEY!

131.   This brings me to a major concern which is on Real estate and Life insurance

If you are investing in real estate or you are in real estate as a business it is important to know about life insurance, how it can benefit you and why you need it. Generally insurance provides money when the policy holder passes away. These insurance policies ranges as high as 100 Million Naira. This money can be used to pay living expenses for the family left behind. There have been cases here in Nigeria where people have been victims and having a LIFE INSURANCE can be an added advantage. It is clear that investors can not only benefit from insurance, but they have a specific need for it. I will advise you choose peace of mind, make time to look at Insurance and treat it as Priority.

Voilà, here we are!

This process seems cumbersome, looking for someone who can help you with all the process? Great! Look no further, Mojisola Afolayan is an Independent Property Advisor and Acquisition Specialist, who helps private clients, and young families in creating wealth through property investment. She does this by providing advisory services via technology, business development and consulting with the aim of ending poverty, empowering women and youth and promoting access to quality education in Nigeria and Africa.

Visit www.mojisolaafolayan.com to know more about her services and how she can be of help to you on your property investment journey.

AFOLAYAN, MOJISOLA MUNIRAT RSV, ANIVS

Mrs Afolayan, Mojisola Munirat nee Yakubu is an Independent Property Advisor and Property Acquisition Specialist, a Certified Real Estate Professional, and award-winning entrepreneur with a focus on promoting sustainability of wealth, property and environment. She is the Principal Partner at Mojisola Afolayan Estates, a real estate solutions company promoting sustainability of property and wealth through advocacy, education and consulting.

Mojisola Afolayan Estates is a real estate solutions company promoting sustainability of property investment and wealth creation through advocacy, education and consulting.

The overall aim is to improve quality of lives and sustainability of communities and cities in Africa by raising awareness of the importance of quality living, fostering property maintenance culture and creation of wealth. The overall aim of this company is linked to the Sustainable Development Goals of the United Nations in order to make the world a better place: SDG1 No Poverty, SDG 9 Industry, Innovation and Infrastructure, SDG11 Sustainable Cities and communities and SDG 15 life on Land and SDG 17 partnership for the Goals

She is an Associate of the Nigerian Institution of Estate Surveyors and Valuers NIESV and an Associate of the Women in Business and Management WIMBIZ and a 2017 mentee under the WIMBIZ mentoring program, the convener of the Blueprint Conference, a Real Estate Investment and Wealth summit which she championed in 2018. She holds a Bachelor of Science in Estate Management from Covenant University where she finished with a second Class upper division. She holds a Comptia Certification as a Project Management professional and holds a professional Master's degree in Transportation Planning and Management from the University of Lagos.

Mojisola sought after her passion for business success with her areas of strength being Business Development and Operations, Clients Retention and Customer Relationship Management with over 10 years of post NYSC work experience in the Banking and Real Estate Industry. She is a wife and mother of three lovely children, result oriented and hard working. She stands for sustainable growth and development, local content development and is a firm believer in a better Africa, where Africans are integral to the solutions of problems in Africa.

References

- Google.com

  https://www.google.com/search?sxsrf=ACYBG NT6TkKKX6ZXfq03QNXDe6zRkvNgKQ%3A1 575504358814&ei=5knoXZ6gMcS-ab7pv_gH&q=what+is+land+&oq=what+is+land+&gs_l=

- NIESV Website https://www.niesv.org.ng/

- COREN Website

- REDAN Website http://redanonline.org.ng/

- NITP Website http://nitpng.com/

- NIQS Website http://niqs.org.ng/

- https://edition.cnn.com/business

- https://www.investopedia.com/terms/i/invest mentadvisor.asp

- https://www.mashvisor.com/

- omo- onile Lawyer